# Contents

Death of the Dinosaurs ..... 4

Fossil Hunting ..... 6

Building a Dinosaur ..... 8

Survivors ..... 10

Insect Survival ..... 12

From the Deep ..... 14

Roaming Reptiles ..... 16

The Tuatara ..... 18

Birds of a Feather ..... 20

Glossary ..... 22

Index ..... 23

Discussion Starters ..... 24

# Features

People have been digging up dinosaur bones for thousands of years. However, they didn't know what the bones were until 200 years ago. Read about the first dinosaur discovery on page 7.

Read all about it—**Giant Crocodile Fossils Found.** Turn to page 16 for news about a crocodile with 7-foot-long jaws!

Turn to **The Tuatara** on page 18 to learn about one of Earth's oldest and most interesting animals.

Animals from long ago were given some very strange names. Turn to page 21 to learn about the meaning behind the name *Archaeopteryx*.

What can scientists tell from fossil footprints? Visit **www.rigbyinfoquest.com** for more about FOSSILS.

# Death of the Dinosaurs

Dinosaurs died out 65 million years ago. Nobody knows for sure what killed them. Some scientists believe that dinosaurs became **extinct** because winters became too cold and summers too hot.

Others believe the dinosaurs died after a large **asteroid** hit Earth and caused huge fires. Clouds of smoke would have blocked out sunlight for months. Without sunlight, plants would have died. Then the dinosaurs would have starved.

When the dinosaurs died, small **mammals** and birds survived because they were able to eat seeds and nuts.

# Fossil Hunting

Everything we know about dinosaurs has come from the study of their **fossils**. Most fossils are bones and teeth, although footprints, eggs, droppings, and skin have also been discovered. To become a fossil, the skeleton of an animal must have been buried under layers of sand or mud. Over time, the sand and mud turn to rock and the bones turn into fossils.

What can scientists tell from fossil footprints?
Visit **www.rigbyinfoquest.com** for more about **FOSSILS**.

**WORD BUILDER**

The word *fossil* comes from the Latin word *fossilis*, which means "dug up." Most fossils are dug up from rock.

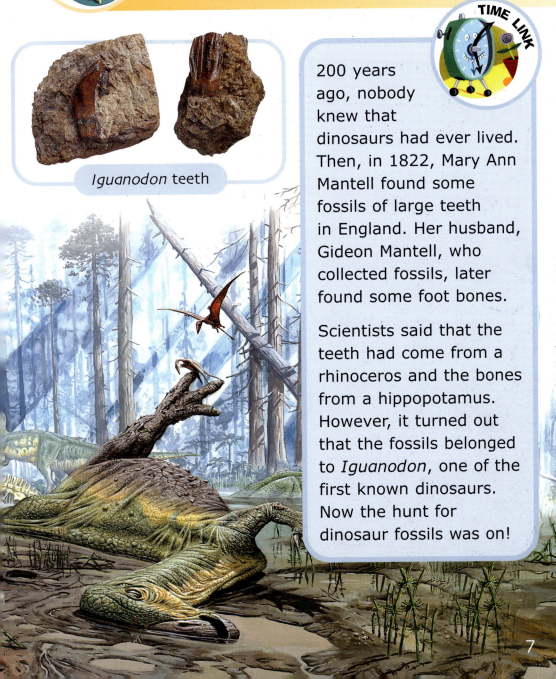

*Iguanodon* teeth

**TIME LINK**

200 years ago, nobody knew that dinosaurs had ever lived. Then, in 1822, Mary Ann Mantell found some fossils of large teeth in England. Her husband, Gideon Mantell, who collected fossils, later found some foot bones.

Scientists said that the teeth had come from a rhinoceros and the bones from a hippopotamus. However, it turned out that the fossils belonged to *Iguanodon*, one of the first known dinosaurs. Now the hunt for dinosaur fossils was on!

# Building a Dinosaur

Scientists can learn a lot from dinosaur fossils. They can tell what the dinosaur ate, how large it grew, how fast it ran, and how it killed its **prey**.

Each fossil is a piece in a dinosaur puzzle, but there are often pieces missing. As scientists put the bones together, they may discover they have found a new type of dinosaur. Around seven new kinds of dinosaurs are discovered each year!

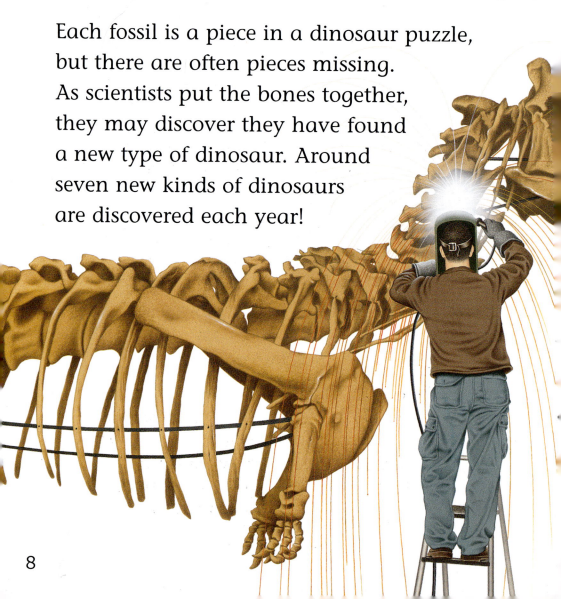

**IN FOCUS**

Fossils are fragile and must be cleaned very carefully. This can take months.

**1**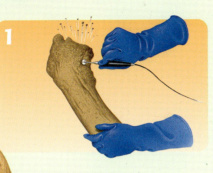

Scientists use tools to remove most of the rock from around a fossil.

**2**

Sometimes they clean the fossil with a sandblaster.

**3**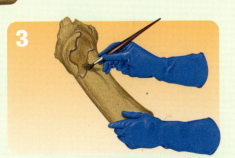

To protect the fossil, they paint it with special glue so it won't fall apart.

**4**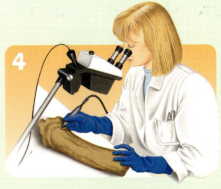

To remove the last small pieces of rock, they work with a microscope and a dentist's drill.

# Survivors

Most of the plants and animals that lived millions of years ago are now extinct. However, the relatives of some plants and animals from long ago are still alive today. They are sometimes called "living fossils."

Nobody knows how these plants and animals have survived. They are all shapes and sizes and can be found in the oceans or on land. Scientists study these survivors to learn more about Earth's history.

The only thing left of these dinosaurs are fossils. However, relatives of the plants they ate are still here today.

Ginkgo leaf fossil

Ginkgo leaves today

Ginkgo leaf fossils from 200 million years ago have fan-shaped leaves like the Ginkgo tree that grows today.

# Insect Survival

You don't need to search far for a living fossil. Many insects today look like the insects that were alive during the time of the dinosaurs, but they are much smaller than their giant relatives.

Today, dragonflies have a wingspan of about 3–4 inches. About 300 million years ago, dragonflies with a wingspan of 2½ feet flew over Earth's **wetlands**. Cockroaches and silverfish are also smaller relatives of giant insects living long ago.

Fossils show that insects have lived on Earth for at least 400 million years.

Cockroaches can survive almost anywhere. They eat many things, including soap and paper.

Some **arachnids** have been around for a long time, too. Fossils show that scorpions haven't changed much in the last 300 million years.

Silverfish

# From the Deep

Our oceans have been full of fish and sea creatures for a very long time. The oldest sharklike fossils are found in rocks around 400 million years old. Today's sharks look a lot like ancient sharks although they are much smaller. Some ancient sharks were up to 50 feet long.

When you compare the tooth of a great white shark (left) with the fossil tooth of a shark from 15 million years ago (right), you can see how big these monsters from the deep must have been.

Starfish fossil

The starfish is a great survivor. There are fossils 400 million years old that look like the starfish you can find in tide pools today.

# Roaming Reptiles

Fossils show that some **reptiles** long ago died out with the dinosaurs. Others survived and became the relatives of today's reptiles.

**IN THE NEWS**

Thursday, November 1, 2001

## Giant Crocodile Fossils Found

The 7-foot-long jaws of this fossilized giant crocodile make the 20-inch jaws of today's crocodile look tiny.

Fossils from a 110-million-year-old crocodile have been found in the Tenere Desert of West Africa. Scientists have studied the fossilized bones and believe that they came from an extinct, giant crocodile. This crocodile was as long as a bus and as heavy as a small whale. It lived in a swamp and ate dinosaurs. Dr. Paul Sereno, a dinosaur expert, said this giant crocodile "would have given dinosaurs nightmares."

# The Tuatara

## What Is a Tuatara?

The tuatara looks like a lizard, but it is actually the last living member of a reptile group that lived with the dinosaurs. Tuataras are relatives of snakes and lizards.

## Where Do Tuataras Live?

When the dinosaurs were alive, tuataras lived in most parts of the world. Today, they can be found only on a few small islands off the coast of New Zealand in the Pacific Ocean. During the day, they sleep in their burrows or rest in the sun. At night, they hunt for food.

New Zealand

## What Do Tuataras Eat?

Tuataras eat earthworms, snails, insects, small lizards, and young birds. They use their sharp teeth to crush and cut their prey.

WORD BUILDER

The New Zealand Maori named the tuatara (*too uh TAH ruh*) for the spikes on its back. In Maori, *tuatara* means "spiny back."

# Birds of a Feather

Some scientists believe that birds are related to small, feathered dinosaurs from long ago. Fossils show that ancient birds and dinosaurs had a similar bone structure.

However, ancient birds did not look much like most of today's birds. *Archaeopteryx* had a reptile's head, a long tail, and claws on the end of its wings.

Some of today's birds behave in a similar way to dinosaurs. The secretary bird of Africa hardly ever flies. Instead, it runs after insects, small reptiles, and mammals in the same way as many dinosaurs did. Baby hoatzins, in South America, use claws on their wings to help them climb trees—just as *Archaeopteryx* did.

**WORD BUILDER**

The name *Archaeopteryx* (*ar kee OP ter iks*) is made of two Greek words. *Archaeo* means "ancient" and *pteryx* means "wing," so the name of this extinct bird means "ancient wing."

Hoatzin

Secretary bird

# Glossary

**arachnid** – an animal with eight legs, a body with two main parts, and no antennae. Spiders, scorpions, mites, and ticks are all arachnids.

**asteroid** – a rocky object in the solar system that orbits the sun and is much smaller than a planet

**extinct** – no longer living. If an animal is extinct, it means that there are no more of that kind of animal alive.

**fossil** – the hardened remains of a plant or animal that lived long ago

**mammal** – an animal that feeds its young on mother's milk. Mammals are warm-blooded and are the only animals that have hair.

**prey** – an animal that is hunted and eaten by another animal

**reptile** – a cold-blooded animal that crawls on its belly or creeps on short legs. Reptiles usually have dry, scaly skin.

**wetland** – an area of land, such as a tidal flat or swamp, that often contains a lot of water

# Index

| | |
|---|---|
| birds | 5, 20–21 |
| crocodiles | 16–17 |
| dinosaurs | 4–8, 10, 12, 16–18, 20 |
| fish | 14 |
| fossils | 6–16, 20 |
| insects | 12–13 |
| mammals | 5 |
| plants | 4, 10–11, 17 |
| reptiles | 16–19 |
| scorpions | 13 |
| starfish | 15 |
| tuataras | 18–19 |

# Discussion Starters

**1** Nobody knows for sure what killed the dinosaurs. Try coming up with some new ideas about why the dinosaurs died out.

**2** Fossils show that insects are much smaller today than they were 300 million years ago. Why do you think this is?

**3** Some ancient animals, such as tuataras, live only in one part of the world. What can we do to help make sure that today's survivors do not become extinct?